Rolf Heimann's
AMAZING MAZES
3

ROLAND HARVEY BOOKS

Roland Harvey Books
92 Bay Street
Port Melbourne
Victoria 3207
Australia

Roland Harvey Books is an imprint of Roland Harvey Studios

First published 1996
Reprinted 1996, 1997

Copyright © Rolf Heimann, 1996

Text designed by Romany Glover

Printed and produced in Hong Kong by South China Printing Co. Ltd

National Library of Australia Cataloguing-in-Publication data

Heimann, Rolf, 1940-

        Amazing mazes 3.

        ISBN 0 949714 46 1

        1. Maze puzzles - Juvenile literature. I. Title

793.73

Introduction

Everybody knows the experience of getting lost.

And everybody knows the pleasure and relief of finding the right path again.

To err is human. Nobody goes through life without ever making a mistake. Taking a wrong path may result in being a few minutes late, or it may even lead to disaster. In this book, Rolf Heimann's third in the 'Amazing' series of maze books, any paths taken will lead to nothing but enjoyment. Sometimes there is only one right path, sometimes there are several that lead to the goal. Explore them all! Rush through the following pages or take your time, but above all, **don't give up!**

Hi, I'm Conny! My name is hidden on every page of this book, even on this one. Can you see it?

1 Mouldy Maze

'Hey, what's with all the toadstools?' asked Tom.

Lila explained, 'This is a very dangerous place. These toadstools were grown by the illustrator himself so that we'll fall on something soft if we should slip. He tried mattresses, but they were rather unsightly. Our task is to make a journey and come back to this very spot here without retracing our steps.'

'Sounds easy,' said Tom.

Lila wasn't so sure. Ben had to make his journey without stepping either up or down, Tom had to go down only, and Lila had to find a path stepping up only. Usually such a thing would have been impossible, but this place was built by a fan of Escher.

Who is Escher anyway?

Ben is the youngest. He does the easiest mazes.

Tom is a little older, so his mazes are harder.

Lila, being the oldest of the three, does the hardest mazes of all.

Collector's item
A major mistake has been made in one of these stamps!
Answer on page 28

'Why do I have the feeling we're being watched?' asked Ben. 'It's downright scary.'
'You're right,' agreed Tom. 'But you know, once you find out just what it is that makes you scared, half your fear is already gone. Let's find all those hidden faces and stare right back at them!'
'Good idea,' agreed Lila, 'but first we must do what we've been sent to do. Exchange these three flags with the old ones of the same colour that have become a bit tattered.'

Hippy group photo 1975
Peachblossom was, as usual, between Rain and Starlight. Tango was then proudly sporting an Afro hairstyle. Jimini was wearing his oversized Army pants. Sunbeam, never without his hat, was behind Rain and Lightfoot. What was the name of the guitar player?
Answer on page 28

Let's face it, they can't face faces!

6

3 Domination

'Correct me if I'm wrong,' said Ben, 'but isn't there only one way to find a path over dominoes, and that is to have dominoes whose ends contain the same number of dots joined up together.'

'Yes, that's the usual way,' agreed Lila, 'and you may use it to make your way to our teddy bear. But there are two other ways as well and they are a bit more difficult. Tom, you must step over the dominoes that are joined together and are the same colour, and I have to step over the dominoes where the colours of the dots match. I'll see you at Teddy Bear Island!'

Would you believe there are 22 differences between the two Egyptian panels above?

Answer on page 28

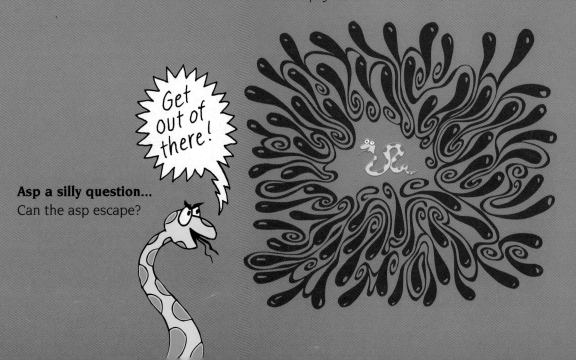

Asp a silly question...
Can the asp escape?

General confusion
Which of the four uniforms matches that worn
by General Sloan-Deppenkirk?
Answer on page 28

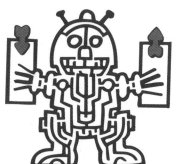

Mini-mazes:
You should be able to
whizz through these in
30 seconds flat!

4 Paint the Tower Red!

'Ah, blue and yellow!' exclaimed Tom, 'my favourite colours!'
'Too bad,' said Lila. 'Our job is to paint the tower red. Ben, you find the paint and Tom, you find a brush. Then both of you have to get up the stairs, any stairs, while I stay on the ground and make my way to the door of the tower. I'll meet you at the tower, okay?'

I hate to say it, but it seems an awful waste of time to build such huge mazes!

5 Problem Pets

The children have been told to feed the animals: Tom has a carrot for the rabbit, Lila has a bone for the dog and Ben has some milk for the cat. Won't they get a surprise when they see the size of the animals!

You know there's a controversy about whether milk is actually good for cats...

JUST GIMME!

Detective Smart has been given these two surveillance photos. Although he has not been told which of the photos was taken earlier than the other, he knows straight away which one it was.
Answer on page 28

Star Express
Time limit: one minute

13

Early bird gets the worm
Can you get the worm in less than one minute?

'Of all the weird places we've been in, this has to be the weirdest,' exclaimed Tom. 'What do we have to do here?'
'It's simple really,' explained Lila. 'We have to meet at the Christmas tree. Don't get dizzy on the way! Oh! And Merry Christmas!'

TAPU

SECRETO

GEHEIM

SEGREDO

立入禁止

RAHASIA

RAHASYAM

GEHEEM · GO HOME

FAA SAINA · ALU ESE

TABOO

GO AWAY!
THERE ARE NO ALIENS*
* it's just swampgas
or a weather balloon

TOP SECRET

TOP SECRET

7 Alien Assignment

Lila, Tom and Ben have made friends with an alien called Xotltoxox who came in search of his brother, Iboki. Iboki had been captured by the US Air Force and kept in a secret facility near Los Pinos Coladas in New Mexico. 'How are we going to get past the guards?' asked a worried Lila. 'Easy,' said Xotltoxox. 'I know a secret spell that turns military guards into harmless ropossums for five minutes. Ropossums are native animals of my home planet, by the way. But five minutes is all we would have. While I watch the ropossums, you, Ben, find our six-legged space dog, Stripo. And Tom, you find the spacecraft, it looks exactly like mine. And Lila, could you look for my identical twin brother? 'Oh, please, please, please,' begged Ben, 'please, please, please, please tell us that secret spell. It would be worth its weight in gold.' 'I can't do that,' said Xotltoxox. 'A secret is a secret is a secret.'

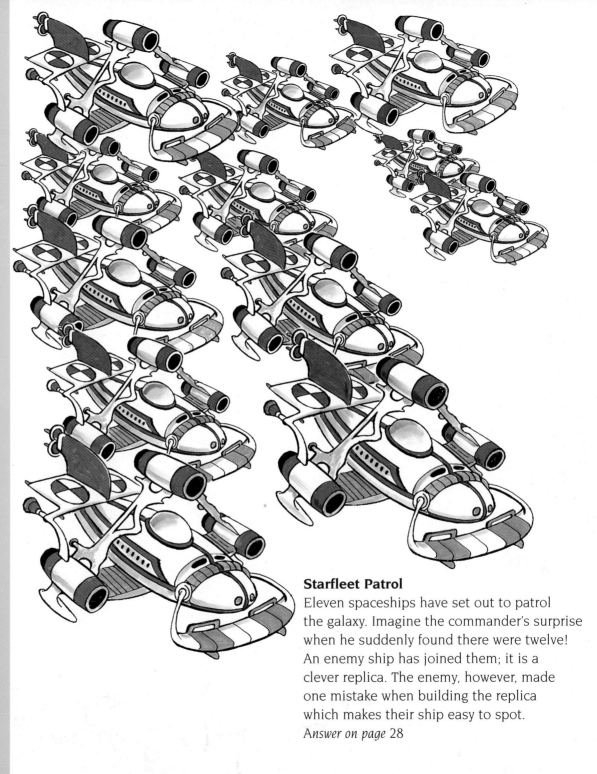

Starfleet Patrol
Eleven spaceships have set out to patrol the galaxy. Imagine the commander's surprise when he suddenly found there were twelve! An enemy ship has joined them; it is a clever replica. The enemy, however, made one mistake when building the replica which makes their ship easy to spot.
Answer on page 28

8 Chamber Chase

Lila, Tom and Ben are not the first to enter the tomb of Queen Ysraphel. Grave robbers have been there before and carried away all the gold and silver. But the children have obtained some secret information about the diaries of the ancient Queen. There are three diaries: one from Ysraphel's childhood, one from her teenage years and one from the time when she reigned as a powerful monarch. Because she had been extremely beautiful as well, newspapers and magazines around the world would pay a fortune for those diaries!

It is not easy, though, to wade one's way through the maze of underground tunnels and chambers and find the chests that match the sacred symbols obtained by the children.

They look scared. Maybe they want their Mummy!

Surrounded by flowers
Sooner or later our bee has to get back to her hive.
Will she find her way out?

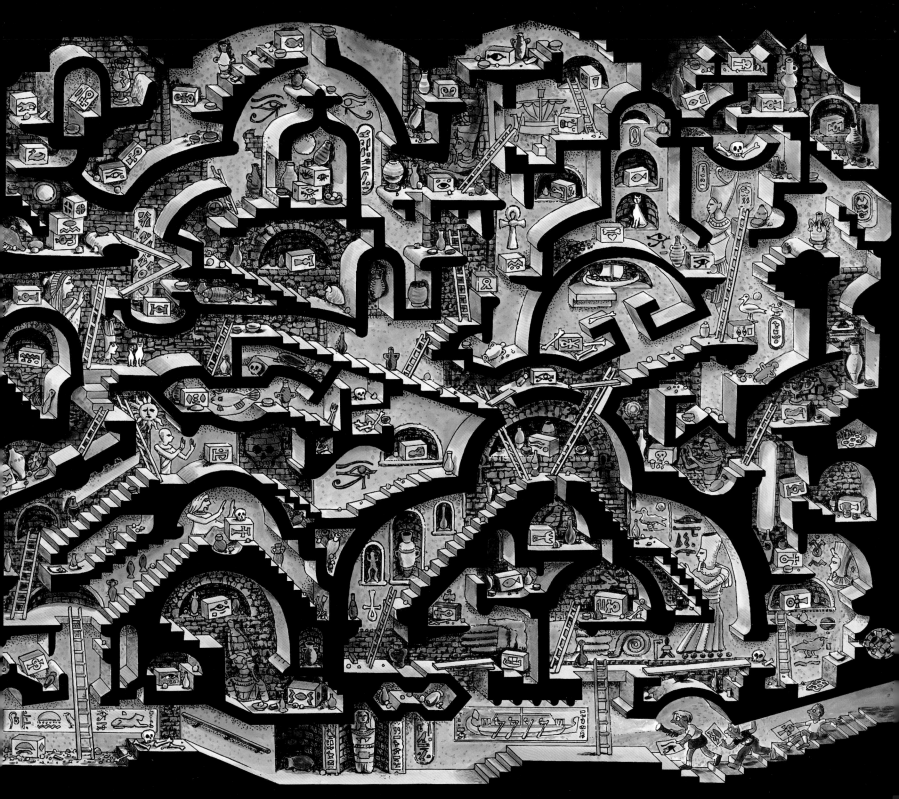

9 Rubbish Retrieval

'Isn't it terrible what people still throw away,' said Lila. 'You'd think they'd never heard of recycling or composting.'

'Well, I must admit I recently threw away a red coathanger just because I didn't like its colour,' confessed Tom.

'Shame on you!' exclaimed Lila. 'Go and find it again! And Ben, have you recently thrown away something as well? Something you shouldn't have?'

'Well, I did throw a boomerang ...' Ben admitted sheepishly.

'Didn't it come back? Did you follow the instructions?'

'They were in a foreign language.'

'Oh, I see,' Lila replied. 'Well, get those things back while I dash across the rubbish tip to retrieve my rucksack. But you must stay on the wooden boards. These rubbish tips can be treacherous.'

A boomerang should be the easiest thing to recycle!

My tail is 3 times longer than that of my cat. If it were 10 cm longer, it would be twice the size of yours. And if my cat's tail were 10 cm shorter, it would be half yours...

Telling tails
Can you work out the length of each creature's tail?

Horseshoe shuffle
Kalamari has passed Foxtrotter and is in the lead while Wild Beauty has slipped to the rear. Hurricane is now positioned between Midnight and Foxtrotter. Which horse is second last?

Answers on page 28

The Giant Malayan Butterflower (*Floribustus incredibus*)
The nectar is sweetest right at the centre of the flower,
so help the butterflies find their way to it.

Only two of these jugs are
identical. Which two are they?
Answer on page 28

10 Bothersome Berries

This task may not seem all that difficult, but it's extremely important to get it right.

The problem is that these three different fruits look so much alike that they are easily mistaken for one another. Ben must find the Giant Blue Wobble Cherry (or *Dulcinosa*) which is excellent for use in Blue Forest cake. Then there is the Big Kibble Berry, an excellent natural remedy for toothache. It's botanical name is *Gloriosis*. Tom must identify that.

And finally there is the extremely dangerous Blue Devil's Apple (*Obnoxia fatalis*), so poisonous that Lila must remove it before anyone comes to harm.

Imagine what could happen if there was a mix up!

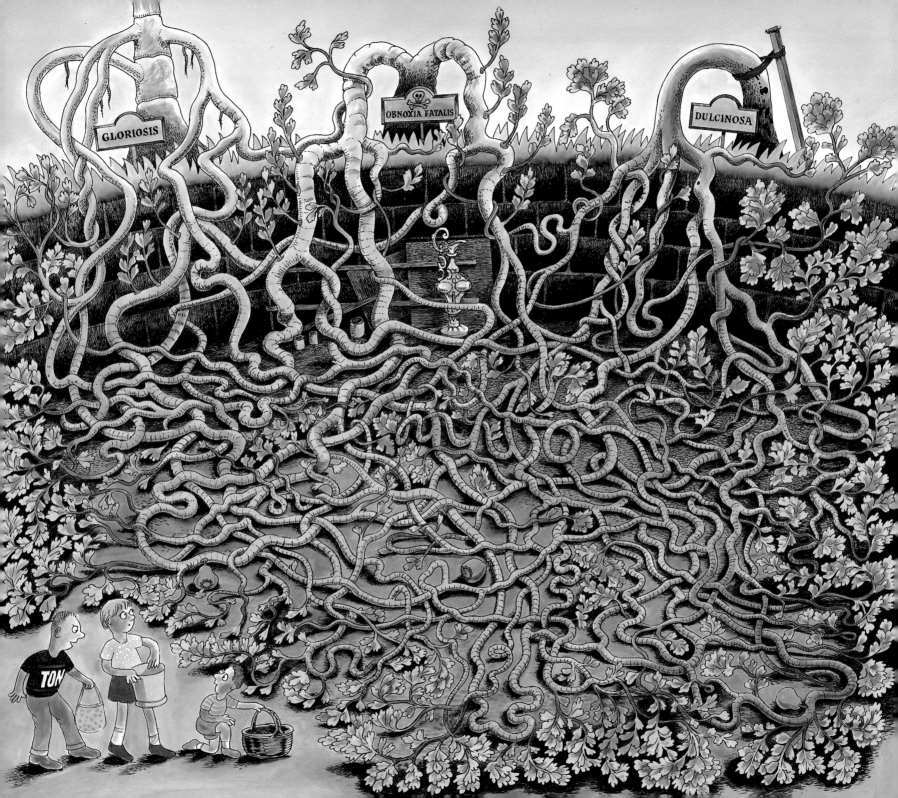

KRONO PARK

CARL NEANDER THAL

PC

TV SNACKS

ARMSTRONG & ALDRIN
S.F.B. MORSE
THOMAS EDISON
O.RVILLE & W.B. WRIGHT
W.K. ROENTGEN
KARL-FRIEDRICH BENZ
GUTENBERG
MONTGOLFIER
A.G. BELL
J. LOGIE BAIRD
1957
1886
1932
1969

11 Timeout

'This place is called Kronopark because we have to find our way in chronological order,' explained Lila. 'Chronological order? I hope it isn't painful,' said Ben sounding a little concerned.

Lila laughed. '*Chronological* means arranged in the correct order according to the time in which something happened. Ben, you guide us on the right path, while Tom puts these names to the monuments they belong to. I'll put these signs with the year on the right spot. It'll be like a walk through history.'

'Wait a minute,' called Tom. 'I've never heard of anyone called Carl Neanderthal!'

'Well,' said Lila, 'maybe that's Lesson Number One—never lose your sense of humour!'

I wonder who invented time?

Answer on page 28

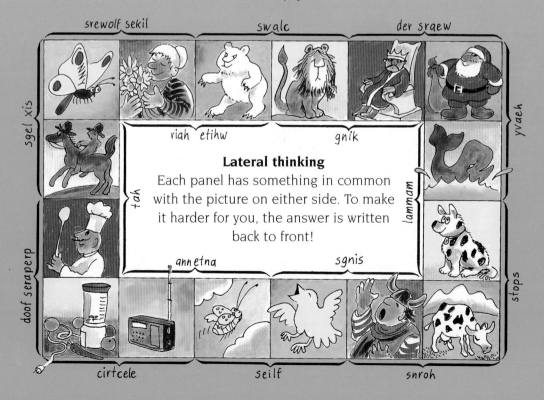

Lateral thinking
Each panel has something in common with the picture on either side. To make it harder for you, the answer is written back to front!

25

Fill in the missing pictures

If you managed to do the lateral thinking exercise on page 25, then you should have no trouble with this one. Again, each picture has something in common with its neighbour. Think about it and try to fill in the three missing pictures.

Answers on page 28

12 In Raptures

'What's so special about wrapping things?' wondered Tom. 'My mother wraps my lunch every day, does that make her an artist?'

'This is about wrapping big things,' explained Lila. 'You see, this fellow Christo has already wrapped the German Reichstag, and some cliffs in Sydney. The bigger the thing, the bigger the art. Now he's wrapped a whole city! Just look out the window. This exhibition here is just some of his earlier work.'

The parcels certainly looked very mysterious indeed, but was it art?

'When I'm grown up,' said Ben, 'I may wrap the whole planet Earth and be the biggest artist ever.'

Lila laughed. 'In the meantime,' she suggested, 'let's find out what these parcels here contain. They are all objects from somewhere in this very book. Ben, you take care of the yellow ones, Tom, you take the blue ones and I'll try to find out what the red ones are.'

Let me OUT!

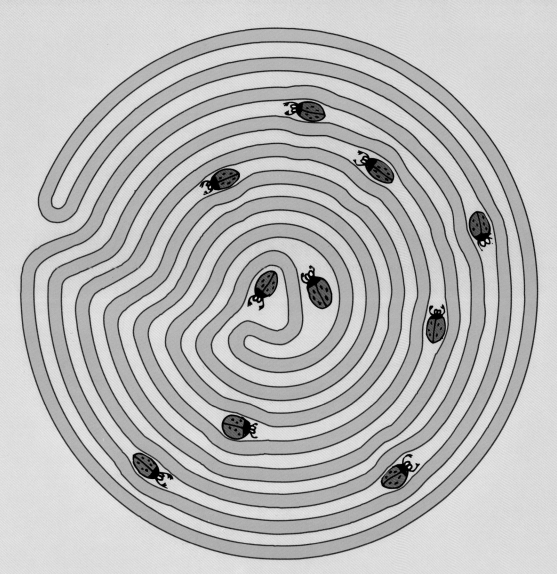

Beetlemania

Which of the beetles will be able to find their way out
and which will stay trapped forever?

You'll only get dizzy following the tracks with your eyes. Here's a tip: Count the lines. An even number means freedom, an odd number means the beetles stay trapped.

Solutions

1 Mouldy Maze

2 Flagging Faces

3 Domination

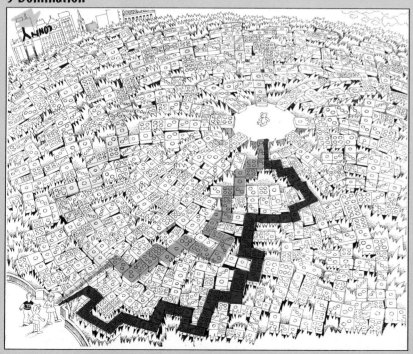

4 Paint the Tower Red!

Ben = red   Tom = blue   Lila = yellow

5 Problem Pets

6 Curly Christmas

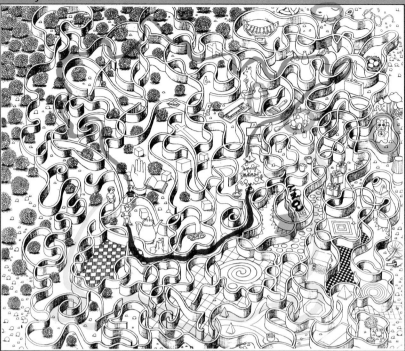

7 Alien Assignment

8 Chamber Chase

Ben = red   Tom = blue   Lila = yellow

9 Rubbish Retrieval

10 Bothersome Berries

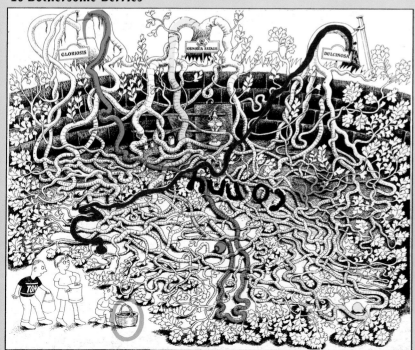

Ben = red   Tom = blue   Lila = yellow

11 Timeout

This is the path through in chronological order.

1 **Club.** Neanderthalers lived about 70,000 years ago, but their more primitive ancestors had already used such simple tools.
2 **Oar.** Oars found in Denmark have been dated to 7000BC.
3 **Wheel.** Wheels were used in Sumer in about 3500BC. Rollers had been used before.
4 **Writing.** In about 2200BC the Minoans used pen and ink for linear writing. Other methods had been used before.
5 **Compass.** Magnetic needles were probably used in China in 1115BC.
6 **Windmill.** About 700BC.
7 **Printing.** Gutenberg was the first European to use moveable type in about 1455.
8 **Microscope.** The Romans had already used glass balls filled with water as magnifying glasses, but in the 17th Century, Leeuwenhoek and others pioneered the building of proper microscopes.
9 **Balloon.** In 1783 the Montgolfier brothers staged the first manned hot air balloon flight.
10 **Steam Locomotive.** In 1804 Trevithick built the first self-propelled locomotive. (George Stephenson's railway opened in 1825.)
11 **Photography.** In 1826 Joseph Nicéphore Niépce made the first photograph. It took 8 hours to expose!
12 **Telegraph.** Invented in 1832 by Morse.
13 **Penny Farthing.** Invented by James Starley in 1871.
14 **Telephone.** Alexander Graham Bell patented the telephone in 1876.
15 **Electric Light.** Patented by Thomas Edison in 1879.
16 **Car.** 1885–first successful petrol-driven car by Karl-Friedrich Benz.
17 **X-rays.** Discovered in 1895 by Roentgen.
18 **Cinema.** In 1895 the Lumiére brothers made improvements on photographic equipment and patented the cinematograph.
19 **Radio.** Patented in 1896 by Marconi.
20 **Plane.** The Wright brothers made the first motorised flight in 1903.
21 **Television.** In 1924 John Logie Baird transmitted the first television pictures.
22 **Satellites.** The first man-made satellite was the Sputnik, sent into orbit by the Russians in 1957.
23 **Moon Walk.** In 1969 Neil Armstrong and Edwin Aldrin were the first men to walk on the moon.
24 **Personal Computers.** Having been improved over a number of decades, computers came into wider use in the 1970s.

12 In Raptures

The green rings will help you find some of the things wrapped for the exhibition. And the green arrows point at my name!

Final feast

Here's a last maze to whet your appetite for more of
Rolf Heimann's amazing mazes. If you don't want to eat the
spaghetti with your fingers, get yourself a fork and spoon.